BASIC TRAINING FOR THE PROPHETIC MINISTRY

STUDY GUIDE

DESTINY IMAGE BOOKS BY KRIS VALLOTTON

Supernatural Ways of Royalty

Basic Training for the Supernatural Ways of Royalty

Developing a Supernatural Lifestyle

Basic Training for the Prophetic Ministry

BASIC TRAINING FOR THE PROPHETIC MINISTRY

STUDY GUIDE

KRIS VALLOTTON

DESTINY IMAGE® PUBLISHERS, INC.
P.O. Box 310, Shippensburg, PA 17257-0310
"Promoting Inspired Lives."

This book and all other Destiny Image and Destiny Image Fiction books are available at Christian bookstores and distributors worldwide.

For more information on foreign distributors, call 717-532-3040.
Reach us on the Internet: www.destinyimage.com.

ISBN 13 TP: 978-0-7684-0738-9

For Worldwide Distribution, Printed in the U.S.A.
9 10 11 12 / 23 22 21 20

Contents

Introduction

Welcome to the adventure of a lifetime!

I've seen the prophetic ministry release captives from bondage and kings into destiny. You, too, are a world-changer! God has put you on earth at this time for a purpose—to demonstrate the life-changing power of Jesus.

My *Basic Training for the Prophetic Ministry Study Guide* will *equip* and *activate* you in the gift of prophecy. This eight-session course is all about giving you practical, nuts and bolts training. There will be risk; your faith will be exercised, but the reward is priceless! The power of the Living God will flow through you to break strongholds, release hope, and change destinies *forever.*

This study guide is designed to go along with the *Basic Training for the Prophetic Ministry* DVD curriculum and the *Basic Training for the Prophetic Ministry* manual. This is a powerful tool for you to use individually or as a group. I encourage you to first watch the DVDs and then go through the daily assignments in this study guide. Each daily assignment is short, challenging you to put into action what you are learning. My aim is to equip you with tools to immediately move in new levels of breakthrough. The weekly Activation Exercises are important for you to "own" the message that is being released. By the end of this training, you will know the heart of the Lord for prophecy and be able to prophesy with confidence.

I believe you will receive a significant impartation through this training. God is preparing you for the places where He is positioning you. Welcome to the journey of risk and adventure. The world is waiting for you!

Breakdown of Sessions

The *Basic Training for the Prophetic Ministry Study Guide* is structured to *equip* and *activate* you in the gift of prophecy. The study guide is divided into eight different sessions. For each session, there is a Group Activity highlighting key points from the DVD teaching and powerful group discussion questions.

In addition, for each session the study guide provides a Daily Prophetic Practice component. These are short sessions designed for daily reflection, building on each other. They cover key prophetic insight, Scripture, and tools for practical application. In total, there are 40 Daily Prophetic Practice sessions designed for your individual growth.

Here is an outline of how each session is presented in the study guide:

Group Activities

1. **Session Summary**: This section provides a brief overview of the topic to be covered and expected learning outcomes.
2. **Video Session**: Watch the video clips specific to each teaching topic. As you listen to the teaching, fill in the selected blanks in the study guide. We also provide space for you to record your own insights.
3. **Discussion Questions**: These are key questions to be covered in your small group or class. If you are going through the curriculum by yourself, we encourage you to still work through the

discussion questions. These questions are critical in the learning process as you communicate in your own words what you have been taught.

4. **Activation Exercise:** This section provides a safe place for you to apply and experiment with your newfound understanding in the prophetic. The Activation Exercises are simple activities designed to help you take a risk.

Daily Prophetic Practice

1. **Prophetic Point:** Each day will begin with a brief key point from the *Basic Training in the Prophetic* DVD series, along with a corresponding Scripture verse.
2. **Make Application:** We explain how the prophetic point is applicable for today.
3. **Take Action**: Here you are provided with some simple reflective questions where you will identify how to apply key prophetic truths to your own life. This activity will help you grow in your ability to discern God's voice and boldly speak what He is saying.
4. **For Additional Study**: Included are links to prophetic resources should you be interested in additional study.

Session One

The Purpose of Prophetic Ministry

There is a significant difference between how prophetic ministry operates in the Old Testament versus the New Testament covenants. To properly prophesy, it is critical for us to understand which covenant we are operating under.

Pursue love, yet desire earnestly spiritual gifts,
but especially that you may prophesy.
—1 Corinthians 14:1

Session Summary

In this session, we will discover *why* God desires for us to prophesy. We will also learn that there is a significant difference between how prophecy functions in the Old Testament versus the New Testament covenants. In the Old Testament, prophecy mainly focused on judgment for sin. However, in the New Testament, prophecy is used to demonstrate the compassionate heart of God, desiring to reconcile people to Himself (see 2 Cor. 5:18).

Basic Training for the Prophetic Ministry manual

Read Chapter 1.

Video Session

How to Operate in New Testament Prophecy

1. Recognize that we live in the *great and glorious,* ________ the *great and terrible.*

2. Find the ________ inside of people, and call it out of them through the prophetic.

3. Call forth the ________ that God has placed inside someone's heart.

Discussion Questions

1. In the past, what was your view of prophetic ministry? Do you believe prophetic ministry is available to all Christians or to only a select few? Explain your answer.

2. What are the main differences in prophetic ministry in the Old Testament versus New Testament covenants? Read Acts 2:17-21 and Malachi 4:5.

3. Why is it important that we know what *day* we are living in?

4. What can happen if we prophesy out of the *wrong day*, believing that we are living in the "great and terrible" Day of Judgment?

5. Explain what it means to find and call out the *gold* in someone.

6. What does this statement mean to you: "Sin is not a secret to sinners; treasure is a secret to sinners."

7. How can calling out "secret treasure" in people actually call them into their divine destiny?

8. Based on what Kris shared about King Saul, how does prophecy have the ability to transform someone into the person he or she was always meant to be?

Activation Exercise: Call Out the Gold!

Goal

Your first prophetic exercise is to find the gold in each other. This activity focuses on speaking words of exhortation and edification to one another; do not call out sins or give words of judgment.

It is important that we do not encourage people from our own natural mind, but from the Holy Spirit. Encouragement is a good thing; however, not all encouragement is prophetic. It is prophecy when the Spirit of God is upon the word, quickening you with His power.

Directions

1. Divide into groups of 2-4 people.
2. Take 5-10 minutes to pray. Listen to the voice of the Holy Spirit and write down what He is saying about each person in your group.
3. Do not overcomplicate the prophecy; if the Holy Spirit shares a single phrase or even one word, share what you receive.
4. After listening in prayer, start to prophesy over each other. Immediately after you give someone a prophetic word, ask them: "Was the word accurate?"
5. Willingly receive feedback! Constructive criticism and correction are important for us to grow in the prophetic. Feedback helps us know if we are hearing from the Holy Spirit correctly and ensures that we are communicating the prophetic word in a way that makes sense.

DAY ONE

The Old Testament Purpose of Prophecy

Therefore the Law has become our tutor to lead us to Christ, so that we may be justified by faith.
—GALATIANS 3:24

Prophetic Point

In the Old Testament, we are judged by our works. In the New Testament, we are judged by Jesus's works.

In the Old Testament, prophecy mainly focused on judgment for sin. The principle role of a prophet was to be a spokesperson for God on earth. They were held to a very high standard for behavior and accuracy in their prophetic words. Prophets were responsible to represent God accurately to the people, which is why the stakes were so high for them. If they prophesied falsely, the consequences could be disastrous.

Make Application

Because we are living under the New Testament covenant now, we cannot hold prophecy to the same standard as in the Old Testament. Not only was prophecy the key way that God spoke to the world about

Himself, but he also used prophetic ministry to render judgment for sins committed.

Under the Old Testament covenant, everything pointed to our need for a Savior. The Old Testament law was a tutor that led us to Jesus, the resurrected Savior who makes available a relationship with God. This is the context in which we need to understand Old Testament prophetic ministry.

Take Action

Explain your understanding of the difference between Old Testament and New Testament prophetic ministry.

Why do you think it is important for you to prophesy from a New Testament covenant perspective rather than an Old Testament covenant perspective?

Recommended Resources

Old Testament Versus New Testament Prophecy

Available at https://shop.ibethel.org/products/old-testament-vs -new-testament -prophecy-8-30am-july-18-2010.

The primary goal of the five-fold ministry is to equip the saints. John the Baptist baptized people for repentance while Jesus baptized for resurrection. When you were baptized, you entered the baptismal tank with a cross but exited with a crown. The old covenant revealed our need for a savior. The prophet's job was to let you know that sin deserved judgment and justice came through judgment. However, the job description for a prophet changed from the old covenant to the new covenant. Under the old covenant, we judge people, while in the new covenant we judge prophecy. In the new covenant, it is a ministry of reconciliation.

DAY TWO

What Day Are You Prophesying From?

The sun will be turned into darkness and the moon into blood, before the great and glorious day of the Lord shall come.
—ACTS 2:20

Behold, I am going to send you Elijah the prophet before the coming of the great and terrible day of the Lord.
—MALACHI 4:5

Prophetic Point

We live in the great and glorious days, not the great and terrible.

The Bible describes two unique days of the Lord—one that is "*great and glorious*" and another that is "*great and terrible.*" It is important that we do not get these two distinct days confused. In the Book of Acts, Peter describes the era of the last days as great and glorious. Referring to a different time than what Peter referenced, the Old Testament prophet Malachi speaks of the great and terrible Day of Judgment *that is yet to come.*

Make Application

It is essential that we know the day that we are living in so that we prophesy in alignment with God's intent. We have no standing to prophesy words of judgment because it is not our place; only God is the Righteous Judge. We have not arrived at the terrible Day of Judgment; that is not the season we are living in. Instead, ever since the Day of Pentecost, we are living in the *great and glorious* last days.

Take Action

Explain why it is important that we know what day we are living in (based on Acts 2:20 and Malachi 4:5).

What do you think happens when people prophesy with the belief that we are living in the *terrible* Day of Judgment? What do their prophecies sound like?

Day Three

Looking for Treasure in Dark Places

But if all prophesy, and an unbeliever or an ungifted man enters, he is convicted by all, he is called to account by all; the secrets of his heart are disclosed; and so he will fall on his face and worship God, declaring that God is certainly among you.
—1 Corinthians 14:24-25

Prophetic Point

Sin is not a secret to sinners; treasure is a secret to sinners.

Many people are scared of receiving prophetic ministry. One common misunderstanding stems from an incorrect reading of First Corinthians 14:24-25 (see above), thinking that the "secrets...disclosed" that Paul discusses refer to our hidden sins. If these Scriptures are read through a wrong lens, people can pick up both a negative stigma toward and the fear of prophetic ministry. They imagine their sins or private challenges becoming public knowledge. This negative, sin-focused word is *not* New Testament prophetic ministry.

Make Application

In First Corinthians 14:24-25, Paul is talking about unbelievers encountering the life-giving power of God though prophetic ministry. When people encounter a prophetic environment, they do not need to be told that they are sinners; they already know that. Instead, New Testament prophetic ministry identifies and calls out the secret potential, destiny, and holiness inside a person. The prophetic ministry has the ability to see someone in their brokenness, but it does not stop there; it sees beyond the current challenge and calls forth God's overwhelmingly good plan. God has such a plan of hope for people! New Testament prophetic ministry is all about reconciling people to God. As we minister in the prophetic under the New Testament covenant, we get to see people the way that God sees them and call them into their greatness!

Take Action

Who are several people in your life the Holy Spirit wants you to call treasure out of? Write down their names below:

Using the names above, ask the Holy Spirit to give you prophetic words for these people. You may receive words right now or you may need to come back to this list once you receive additional revelation. I encourage you to make this a regular practice in life, especially with those who are not in a relationship with Jesus Christ yet. Calling out the treasure in a person's life opens a door for them to see the heart of the Father toward them.

Day Four

Call Out the Image of God in People

Then God said, "Let Us make man in Our image, according to Our likeness."
—Genesis 1:26

Prophetic Point

Inside of every sinner is the image of God that we get to identify and call forth.

Our aim is to look for the image and likeness of God inside of people—and speak to that. Believer or not, all people were created in God's image. Sin brought corruption and infection to human nature, but did not change the fact that all people were fashioned by the Creator in His image. As we prophesy, it is important to start from this foundational truth.

Make Application

It is essential to speak to the image of God in people because it reminds them of who they were created to reflect. Sinners are constantly aware of their shortcomings. Often, their experience with the church is negative because the community of faith tends to focus more on who they are *not* rather than who they are. This is not to say that all people enter the Kingdom of God just because they were created in God's image. However, when we tell people that they are the glorious masterpiece of a good Father, it is a reminder of who God has made them to be. This may be the very message that the Holy Spirit uses to prompt them into a relationship with Jesus. Amazingly, we get to participate in this process!

Take Action

How can reminding people that they were created in God's image and likeness actually prophesy to them?

Describe how the revelation of God as Creator and Father brings hope to those who are not in relationship with Him.

DAY FIVE

Prophecy Calls People into Destiny

Then the Spirit of the Lord will come upon you mightily, and you shall prophesy with them and be changed into another man.
—1 SAMUEL 10:6

Prophetic Point

Prophecy does not just call out the future in one's life; it has the ability to transform them into the person they were always meant to be.

With a pauper's view of his own worth, Saul could not assume the position as King of Israel. It would have destroyed him and the people he was called to lead. But Samuel the prophet told Saul of the greatness that resided within him. Then, shrinking back, Saul responded, "*Am I not a Benjamite, of the smallest of the tribes of Israel, and my family the least of all the families of the tribe of Benjamin? Why then do you speak to me in this way?*" (1 Samuel 9:21). The future king suffered from an inferiority complex. It was very difficult for him to receive the prophetic announcement that he was called to be king. To break this pauper mentality, Samuel gave Saul instructions to meet a group of prophets. In their midst, the Spirit of God came upon Saul and he was "*changed into another man*" (1 Samuel 10:6).

Make Application

Prophecy sees the "God-breathed" destiny inside of people and calls it forth. Saul could not grasp who he had been called to be; therefore, his negative mentality was an inhibitor in Saul's life and needed to be changed. This is why he had to go to the prophets. In their midst, words of prophecy awakened Saul to be the man he was created to be. Prophecy helps us embrace the incredible destiny God has prepared for us.

Take Action

Do you know any *Sauls* in your life? These are people who you can see are called to greatness, but they do not seem to know who they are. Write down their names below:

Ask the Holy Spirit to give you prophetic words for each person, specifically speaking to their God-breathed destiny like Saul's example of *being changed into another man*. You do not need to remind them of their issues or sins. They are aware of what inhibits them from being who God has called them to be. Your job is to speak to that "other man" or "other woman." By prophesying to their greatness, the Holy Spirit awakens them to their godly destiny.

For Additional Study

The Role of New Testament Prophets

Available at https://shop.ibethel.org/products/the-role-of-the-new-testament-prophets-11-00am-october-17-2010.

Old Testament vs. New Testament Prophecy

Available at https://shop.bethel.org/products/old-testament-vs-new-testament-prophecy-11-00am-july-18-2010.

SESSION TWO

The Essential Parts of Prophecy

We must be able to identify the different spiritual components that work together, making prophecy effective in our lives. When New Testament prophetic ministry is functioning, there will be certain characteristics that help us clearly recognize its validity.

Now concerning spiritual gifts, brethren,
I do not want you to be unaware.
—1 CORINTHIANS 12:1

Session Summary

God does not want us to be ignorant about the spirit realm. If we do not know how the spirit realm operates, then it will be challenging for us to flow in the different gifts of the Holy Spirit. There are key guiding principles that govern how the unseen world works. If we apply these principles, then we will start activating the supernatural power of the Holy Spirit in our lives.

Basic Training for the Prophetic Ministry manual

Read Chapter 2.

Video Session

1. God wants you to be aware of and ________ about spiritual gifts.
2. The gifts of the Spirit need to be centered in ________.
3. We are to earnestly ________ spiritual gifts.
4. Prophecy convicts us of the ________ that we all fell short of.

Two Expressions of the Prophetic:

1. Foretelling: Telling the ________.
2. Forthtelling: ________ the future.

- Prophecy sees dry bones and ________ to them as God sees them.

Discussion Questions

1. What does it mean to be informed about the *spirit realm*?
2. How do we receive the gifts of the Spirit? (Read 1 Corinthians 14:1).
3. Read First Corinthians 14:3. Explain the three-part definition of New Testament prophecy:
    a. to edify
    b. to exhort
    c. to console
4. How does prophecy convict us of the glory that we fell short of?
5. Explain the two expressions of the prophetic and how they are different from each other.

   a. foretelling

   b. forthtelling

6. Describe the three parts of prophecy.
7. What is the difference between *interpretation* and *application*?
8. Why is it important to leave the *application* of a prophecy to God's direction (and not try to add in our own ideas of how a prophetic word *should* be applied)?

Activation Exercise: Ask for the Gifts

Goal

The key to start flowing in the gifts of the Holy Spirit is *to ask*. Remember, these are gifts—not rewards. They are not earned by our merits; they are simply received by those who ask. Before moving forward in the following sessions, it is important that everyone is hungry to receive and operate in the gifts.

Your group leader will guide everyone in a prayer that expresses this desire for the gifts. Hunger is the key to positioning yourself to receive more.

Directions

1. Pray as a group and ask for the gifts of the Holy Spirit.
2. The key is *receiving*, not striving.
3. Hold out your hands like you are receiving a gift. This is a prophetic act that expresses the attitude of the heart. It is not about the eloquence of your prayers; it is not about how long you pray or how spiritual you sound. God is looking for those who simply ask and then set their hearts to receive from Him by grace.

4. Your group leader will open in prayer. Next, everyone can:
   a. Lift your voices together, asking for the release of the prophetic in your lives.

   b. Leaders can invite group participants to pray for each other. One technique is to have individuals lay hands on the shoulders of the people to their left and right.

   c. Remember to be specific and intentional in your prayers. You are not asking God, "If it be Your will, can I please move in the gifts of the Spirit?" It *is* His will that you ask Him, and it is His desire to give you the gifts.

   d. Following the time of prayer, share what you are experiencing with your group. Specifically communicate if you receive a prophetic word or word of knowledge.

Remember, this is a safe place where the gifts of the Spirit can be practiced.

Day Six

Learn How the Spirit Realm Works

Now concerning spiritual gifts, brethren,
I do not want you to be unaware.
—1 Corinthians 12:1

Prophetic Point

Paul taught the Corinthian church on matters of the spirit realm, not just about the gifts of the Holy Spirit.

Reading through First Corinthians chapters 12 and 14, it is commonly thought that Paul is specifically addressing the nine gifts of the Holy Spirit. Even though he spends time explaining about the gifts, one main objective for First Corinthians 12 is to unveil how the spirit realm operates. Understanding the principles of how the Spirit realm works is foundational for every believer who desires to move in any of the gifts of the Holy Spirit.

Make Application

First Corinthians 12 and 14 were written to inform Christians about the spiritual realm and gifts of the Holy Spirit. Paul's motivation is that believers would not be ignorant or uninformed. If we live in ignorance to the spirit realm, we are not capable of interacting with it appropriately. Likewise, if we are ignorant to the reality of the gifts of the Holy Spirit, we will not step out in faith, requesting them from God, nor benefiting from their operation in our lives. One of the first hurdles many Christians need to cross in order to move in the prophetic is to recognize that the gifts of the Holy Spirit *are* in operation and that God does *not* want us to be unaware of the spirit realm.

Take Action

Why do you think Paul wanted believers to be informed about the spirit realm and the gifts of the Holy Spirit?

Based on what you learned in Session 2, what are the main ways that you can begin to move in the gifts of the Holy Spirit?

I encourage you to keep track of how the Holy Spirit moves in your life *as you ask Him* to manifest His gifts through you. You can keep a separate journal, or you can use this study guide to document what He is doing in your life.

Day Seven

Your First Step toward Moving in the Gifts

Pursue love, yet desire earnestly spiritual gifts, but especially that you may prophesy.
—1 Corinthians 14:1

Prophetic Point

You express your desire for spiritual gifts by asking.

Everything that we learn about the spirit realm has a practical application. It is not just to gather more knowledge or information. The fact remains that the prophetic gifts have a very practical, everyday use in the lives of Christians. The key to unlocking them is through asking.

Make Application

Again, the gifts of the Holy Spirit are *gifts*, not rewards. You do not earn them through good works, but by simply asking God for the gifts and He will release them to you. There are many Christians who *believe* in spiritual gifts, but have not taken the next step to *earnestly desire* the gifts' operation in their lives. This step to *earnestly desire* is where information becomes actualized. Do not be content to live with just a theological understanding of spiritual gifts, but ask God to release them to you so they can flow *through* you.

Take Action

Ask God to release the gifts of the Holy Spirit in your life—specifically, the prophetic gifts ("*but especially that you may prophesy*"). Because Paul emphasizes prophecy as an important gift, you should earnestly desire for the prophetic to flow in your life.

Write out a simple prayer below to specifically ask for the prophetic gifts to start operating in your life. Continue to pray this with hunger, expecting that God will answer.

Prophetic Journal

This week, I want you to write down how the Holy Spirit is beginning to work in your life through prophetic gifts. Celebrate each step in your progress! You may hear God's voice more clearly or in a different way than before.

Day Eight

The Three Purposes of Prophecy

But one who prophesies speaks to men for edification and exhortation and consolation.
—1 Corinthians 14:3

Prophetic Point

The gift of prophecy or the office of a prophet should never replace your personal relationship with Jesus.

Prophecy is intended to build up (edify), to call someone near to God (exhort), and to comfort (console). In the past, there was the belief that prophetic ministry existed to call out people's secret sins and then parade their brokenness in front of others. This is a gross abuse of New Testament prophetic ministry. Paul explains the three-fold purpose of prophecy in the First Corinthians passage above. This should be our standard for evaluating legitimate prophetic ministry. If a prophet or prophetic word does not meet these three criteria, we have reason to be wary.

Make Application

It is essential to know that prophecy, including both receiving and giving a word, does not replace the need to develop an ongoing personal relationship with Jesus. It is important for prophecy to meet three biblical criteria; it is all about people being built up, exhorted, and consoled *in God*. Fundamentally, *exhorting* is to call a person near to God. A key test of true prophetic ministry is its ability to draw people closer to God. If a prophet or prophetic word creates a sense of distancing from God or makes a person the focus rather than Him, you have reason to question the word.

Take Action

Describe what you previously thought about the gift of prophecy. What new insights did you learn about prophecy through this week's session?

How can prophecy bring people closer to God? Explain.

Prophetic Journal

This week, write down how the Holy Spirit is working in your life through the prophetic gifts. Celebrate each step in your progress. You may start to hear God's voice more clearly, in a different manner, or be stirred to share a word with someone.

DAY NINE

Prophecy Convicts of Original Glory

For all have sinned and fall short of the glory of God.
—Romans 3:23

Prophetic Point

"We've heard a bit about original sin, but not nearly enough about original glory, which comes before sin and is deeper to our nature."
—John Eldredge, *Waking the Dead*

Prophecy is the way that people hear about their original glory. Most people already know they are sinful. They are aware of the chasm that exists between perfection and imperfection, feeling the distance that separates them from God. Separation is not God's desire or intention. Though many are familiar with sin, few understand about the glory that God desires to bring them back into. As we prophesy, we are telling people of God's will for them to live in His glory. We are calling out to the deepest parts within them—the depths that long to be restored to relationship and this original glory. In Eden, man and woman lived in God's glory. This was their normal environment. Today, much of our focus is directed toward the fall of man rather than recapturing a vision for original glory. The prophetic ministry actually calls forth the *image and likeness of God* in someone.

Make Application

When we prophesy, people come into awareness of original glory. They are given a glimpse of what should be the norm for every person in the world—living in the glory of God. In Numbers 14:21, Scripture tells us that God's desire is for the earth to be covered by His glory. This happens through partnership. God partners with people who are redeemed and filled with His glory. It has been His desire for us, in turn, to carry His glory to the ends of the earth.

Take Action

Why do you think it is important to tell people about their original glory? How does hearing this message change someone's life?

Ask the Holy Spirit for clear, practical ways that you can share this message of "original glory" with people in your life.

In the space below, write down the language that the Holy Spirit gives you about original glory. It is important for us to be able to clearly explain this message, because it is missing and so needed in the world today.

Prophetic Journal

Write down the people who come to mind who need to hear this *original glory* message. Start by praying for them; listen for what the Holy Spirit wants you to share with them.

The Three Parts of Prophecy

Prophetic Point

When God stops talking, we should too.

There are three parts of prophecy that we need to be mindful of:

1. **Revelation**: *What is God saying?* The Holy Spirit speaks to our human spirits and we receive prophetic insight. God reveals something to us.

2. **Interpretation**: *What does it mean?* We ask the Lord what the revelation means. It is important that we do not interpret the revelation using our natural human wisdom; rather, leave the work of interpretation to the Holy Spirit.

3. **Application**: *What do we do about what the prophecy means?* We put the prophecy into action and apply it to our lives. We need the Holy Spirit's guidance; otherwise we may apply a prophecy based on our assumption rather than direction of the Lord.

Make Application

As we gain clarity on how prophecy works, we can identify where we are in the prophetic process.

When you receive a prophetic word, wait on the Lord to provide the interpretation and application of the word in your life. Sometimes, people who are releasing a prophetic word can step beyond their revelation and insert *their* ideas of what the interpretation or application should be. Remember, the Lord is the source of understanding.

Likewise, when we are the one giving a prophecy, we need to take care not to overstep our bounds. When God stops talking, we should too! If all He gives us is the revelation, share that and no more. However, if He gives you the interpretation or application of the word, share it. There is a strong likelihood that the person to whom you are prophesying to will receive from the Holy Spirit the interpretation or application. Be obedient to what the Holy Spirit is saying.

Take Action

Explain the difference between the interpretation and application of a prophetic word.

Why do you think it is important to leave prophetic interpretation and application up to God's leading?

For Additional Study

Prophecy and Prophets—Part 1

Available at https://shop.ibethel.org/products/prophecy-prophets-part-1-10-30am-february-16-2014.

Session Three

Hearing God's Voice and Learning God's Language

God's first language is not English. Neither is it Hebrew, Greek, nor Aramaic. He is multi-lingual and communicates through a variety of different ways. The more we acquaint ourselves with the different ways that God speaks, the more clearly we will hear His voice.

My sheep hear My voice, and I know them, and they follow Me.
—John 10:27

Session Summary

God is always communicating. God is multi-lingual; He uses many different ways to communicate with us. Unfortunately, many Christians struggle with this fact because they claim to *not* hear God's voice. We think that God is silent when, in fact, we do not understand some of the various ways that He communicates with us. The more informed we become about God's different "languages," the more we position ourselves to recognize His voice.

In this session, you will be introduced to various ways through which God speaks with His people. We can only prophesy to the degree that we hear and discern God's voice.

Basic Training for the Prophetic Ministry manual

Read Chapters 3–4.

Video Session

Four Voices that Speak from the Spirit Realm:

1. Our ________ spirit
2. The ________ Spirit
3. ____________ spirits
4. ____________

Ways that God Speaks to His People Today:

1. ______________
    a. Visions of the ____________
    b. ____________ visions
2. ____________
3. ____________
4. ____________
5. ____________ of spirits

Discussion Questions

1. What do you think the following statement means: "God is multi-lingual."
2. List some of the ways that people *commonly* hear God's voice.
3. Based on what Kris shared in Session 3, what surprised you most about some of the different ways that God speaks?

4. How can you learn to recognize God's voice *better*?
5. List the four voices that speak to us from the spirit realm.
6. How is the human spirit different from the Holy Spirit?
7. Describe some of the different ways that God speaks to people based on what you watched in Session 3.
8. Ask the group members to share about times when they heard God speaking through some of the different ways that Kris mentioned.*

*__Note__: The purpose of having participants share testimonies is to create an environment of faith and expectancy. We receive in proportion to our faith. If we do not have faith that God will speak to us through visions, dreams, trances, etc., then we will not have the expectation to see them in our lives. Faith and expectation are keys to breakthrough!

Activation Exercise: Practice Hearing God's Voice

- Ask the Holy Spirit to open your senses to the different ways that He communicates.
- Take 10 to 15 minutes of quiet time to wait upon the Lord.
- *Share* about how God spoke to you during this time.
- If you *did not* feel like God spoke to you during this time, be in an attitude of expectancy all week. God wants to speak to you in new, different ways. Keep a journal of God's communication with you over the days ahead. You will find space in this study guide to write down how God communicates with you and what He says.

Day Eleven

Learning the Languages of God

My sheep hear My voice, and I know them, and they follow Me.
—John 10:27

Prophetic Point

God is multi-lingual; He is not limited to speaking in one specific way.

God does not have *one* primary way of speaking to His people. He is Spirit and communicates with people through a Spirit-to-spirit process. Many of us have different ideas of what God's voice *should* sound like. Some expect a booming audible voice like Samuel experienced in First Samuel 3:1-10. Others are always looking for the still small witness like Elijah heard in First Kings 19:12. While God does occasionally speak audibly and the Holy Spirit does often communicate with us through an inward witness, those are not the only exclusive ways that God speaks.

Make Application

When we are only looking for a few specific ways that the Holy Spirit speaks to us, we miss out on other ways that He might want to talk to us. It is time to broaden and expand our spiritual understanding of how to hear God's voice. One thing is for sure: God wants you to hear His voice. Communicating with Him was never meant to be a mystery for believers!

Take Action

What are different ways that *you* have heard God speak to you in the past? List these below:

Based on what Kris shared in the video session, what are some *new ways* that you would like to hear God speak to you?

You have now learned that God is multi-lingual. Be in a state of expectation for new ways that God wants to communicate with you this week. Be continually asking the Holy Spirit for discernment in how He wants to speak to you and for Him to prepare your spirit to receive from Him.

Prophetic Journal

Journal how God is speaking to you this week:

Learning God's Voice Is a Process

For those who are led by the Spirit of God are the children of God.
—Romans 8:14 NIV

Prophetic Point

We learn to recognize God's voice through experience and having constant interaction with Him.

Learning to discern God's voice is a process; it does not just happen in an instant. Do not allow this to discourage you. You will become familiar with God's voice through having interaction with Him over time. Here is your assurance: As a son or daughter of God, it is your inheritance to be led by the Spirit of God. Although it may be a process to learn *how* God speaks, it is something God wants you to grow into. He wants you to hear His voice even more than you do!

Make Application

Enjoy the journey of discovering how God speaks to you. Do not get down on yourself or beat yourself up. Most importantly, just because you do not *feel* like you hear God, do not assume that He is not speaking. The key to hearing from God is by fine-tuning our ability to discern His voice. Often, this involves unlearning some of the assumptions that we have adopted over the course of our Christian lives. We *expect* God to speak in a certain way; therefore, we have developed an ability to discern when He speaks in those predetermined ways.

Take Action

Ask: *Holy Spirit, what are some different ways that You want to speak to me?*

Wait quietly before the Lord and see what He says. One thing I encourage you to do is review different accounts in the Bible where God communicates with people. Write down the various methods that God speaks through these biblical accounts.

Prophetic Journal

Journal how God is speaking to you this week:

Day Thirteen

Four Different Voices

Beloved, do not believe every spirit, but test the spirits to see whether they are from God, because many false prophets have gone out into the world.
—1 John 4:1

Prophetic Point

We should not have more faith in the devil's ability to deceive us than in God's ability to lead us.

Confusion is one thing that inhibits many believers from hearing God's voice. God is not the author of confusion; it is our enemy that brings confusion into the equation. The devil wants us to live in a state of confusion about who is speaking: *Is it God? Is it an evil spirit? Is it my human spirit? Are angels talking with me?* The key to recognizing God's voice is by knowing His nature. When we can clearly see the nature of God in the message we are receiving, we can be confident that the message reflects God's heart. Later on, we will look at different ways to judge and evaluate prophecy. Right now, it is important to know that there are four different voices that are communicating to us from the spirit realm.

Make Application

Do not be alarmed that we have four voices speaking to us. As spiritual beings, it is only normal that we have the ability to pick up on different voices present in the spirit realm. This is not scary or spooky; it is just part of the Christian life. However, when we do not identify the source of the message we are receiving, we can live in confusion and fear, not recognizing *who* is speaking to us. If we are fearful and confused about the spirit realm, we can accidentally dismiss some of the more supernatural ways that God speaks—through visions, dreams, trances, signs, and wonders. *If* an evil spirit speaks to you, do not listen! Do not accept what they are saying as it is contrary to God's good heart. Do not have more confidence in the enemy's ability to deceive us than God's ability to lead us. When we understand that there are four different voices speaking to us, we are able to more clearly identify and discern what messages to receive or not to receive.

Take Action

Describe the difference between the Holy Spirit and your human spirit. Why is this distinction important to know, especially when you are getting ready to share a prophetic word?

Why is discernment so important when listening for the Holy Spirit?

Prophetic Journal

Journal how God is speaking to you this week:

Day Fourteen

Visions and Dreams

"And it shall be in the last days," God says, "that I will pour forth of My Spirit on all mankind; and your sons and your daughters shall prophesy, and your young men shall see visions, and your old men shall dream dreams."

—Acts 2:17

Prophetic Point

It is our privilege to hear the Holy Spirit through visions, dreams, signs, and wonders; this supernatural access has been available since the Day of Pentecost, ushering in the *last days* period. In order to hear God, we often need to expand our understanding of how He speaks. Remember, He does not communicate exclusively through words. His form of speech is not tied to our normal human concept of communication. As the Psalmist explains, God even speaks through creation:

> *The heavens are telling of the glory of God; and their expanse is declaring the work of His hands. Day to day pours forth speech, and night to night reveals knowledge. There is no speech, nor are there words; their voice is not heard* (Psalm 19:1-3).

Make Application

Creation declares the glory of God, even though human speech is not utilized. In the same way that creation is an instrument of God's voice, God wants to speak through visions and dreams. Ask the Holy Spirit to help you hear His voice at a different level. Pray: *Lord, help me to listen at Your frequency.* Too often, we are striving to hear God in the same way that we would listen to a fellow human being. Visions and dreams are one way of God reminding us that His speech is far superior to only using mere words.

Take Action

Explain the difference between a vision of the mind and an open vision.

Why is it important for you to know that not all dreams come from God?

Prophetic Journal

Journal how God is speaking to you this week:

Day Fifteen

Trances and Other Supernatural Experiences

But he (Peter) *became hungry and was desiring to eat; but while they were making preparations, he fell into a trance.*
—Acts 10:10

Prophetic Point

The devil is not an inventor or creator; he is a copier. The devil only copies and counterfeits what is valuable.

Immediately, when some Christians hear the word *trance*, they push back: "That's not of God; that's New Age!" However, in the Book of Acts the apostle Peter receives his instruction to preach the Gospel to the Gentiles through a trance. At this point in history, God reveals His desire to adopt these previously excluded people into His redemptive plan.

While in a trance, a person may be physically present, but mentally and/or spiritually they are in a different place. Even though this is a practice used by the occult and New Age adherents, it has its origins in the Kingdom of God. In the same way that fortune-tellers, tarot card readers, and psychics are counterfeits of the prophetic, the demonic has counterfeited the trance from God's original intention.

Make Application

Many believers have a difficult time embracing trances, signs and wonders, or other supernatural means of communication as from God. Because of this, we have closed off ourselves to the possibility of God actually speaking to us through these different methods. We can become so fearful of being deceived that we miss out on what God wants to say. Our image of a deceiving devil becomes greater than our understanding of the power of the Holy Spirit, who promises to lead us into all truth (see John 16:13). We need to be looking at the fruit or result of our experiences. If we go into a trance, see a vision, or have some kind of supernatural encounter, the result of the encounter should reflect the *fruit of the Spirit* as defined in Scripture. These encounters should advance the Kingdom of God. They should reflect the nature and character of Jesus. They should promote Heaven's agenda of seeing the earth filled with God's glory. The *means* that God uses to communicate His message could challenge our personal comfort zone; however, if the result is the advancement of His Kingdom and the fruit of the Spirit is present, we must be open to new avenues of God's speech to us.

Take Action

Read Acts 10:1–11:18. Because of Peter's trance, what fruit is produced?

Why do you think it is important for you to be open to unusual ways that God speaks, even if they are outside of your comfort zone?

Prophetic Journal

Journal how God is speaking to you this week:

For Additional Study

Ministering in the Spirit of Elijah

Available at https://shop.ibethel.org/products/ministering-in-the-spirit-of-elijah.

When God Is Silent

Available at https://shop.ibethel.org/products/when-god-is-silent-6-00pm-november-28-2010.

SESSION FOUR

How to Judge and Evaluate Prophetic Words

People tend to take one of two approaches to prophetic ministry—either complete rejection of this ministry or no restraints toward it. When we completely reject prophecy, we are despising it. Conversely, when we do not practice discernment, we are not examining everything carefully as outlined in Scripture. It is important for us to follow the guidelines in Scripture if we are going to operate correctly in prophetic ministry.

Do not quench the Spirit; do not despise prophetic utterances. But examine everything carefully; hold fast to that which is good.
—1 THESSALONIANS 5:19-21

Summary

In order to operate in the prophetic accurately or create a healthy prophetic culture, it is important to be grounded in what Scripture says about evaluating and judging prophetic words. Because we are living under the New Covenant, we are no longer judging people; we are judging their prophetic words. If someone gives an incorrect prophetic word, it does not make him or her a false prophet.

Basic Training for the Prophetic Ministry manual

Read Chapter 5.

Video Session

Keys to Evaluating a Prophetic Word:

1. Identify the ________ of the prophetic word.
2. Develop a ________ gate for inaccurate prophetic words.
3. Evaluate the ________ of the prophetic word and what it produces in your life.

How to Judge and Evaluate Prophetic Words:

1. Make sure the prophetic word is *not* ________ .
2. Your spirit needs to bear ________ to the prophetic word.

Discussion Questions

1. Read First Thessalonians 5:19-21. Why do you think Paul gives instructions for the people *not* to despise prophecy?
2. How can you identify the source of a prophetic word?
3. Who is able to discern and evaluate the source of prophetic words? Is this available exclusively to a select group of people or can all believers participate?
4. Describe what Kris meant by "developing a refuse gate." Why is this especially important if you want to build a healthy prophetic culture?
5. What are ways that you can identify whether or not a prophetic word is accurate? Ask people in the group to share their testimonies of receiving an *inaccurate* prophetic word, how they knew it was wrong, and how they responded.
6. Explain the difference between biblical, extra-biblical, and anti-biblical.

7. How can your spirit receive a prophetic word even if the word does not make sense to your mind?
8. What does it look like for your spirit to *bear witness* with a prophetic word?

Activation Exercise: Practice Giving Prophetic Words and Share Honest Feedback

This activity is similar to Week One. This is intentional. Be sure to compare this exercise to Week One, evaluating if you notice improvement in your ability to hear God's voice and deliver an accurate prophetic word.

Here are a few ground rules for this exercise to be successful:

- Remember, *everyone* is learning; consider this a laboratory for the gifts of the Spirit.
- Show grace and honor toward each other while also being open and honest. If the prophetic word is not accurate, you need to share this feedback.
- This exercise can be done in a few different ways:
    - One person can volunteer to go in the middle of the room and be the person whom everyone prophesies over.
    - Break up into groups of two (men with men, women with women) and prophesy over each other.
- If you receive a prophetic word, write it down for further evaluation throughout the week.

***Note**: You may receive a word that does not resonate with your mind but, at the same time, is not rejected by your spirit. These are prophecies to "put on the shelf" and ask the Holy Spirit for greater clarity.

Don't Quench the Holy Spirit

Do not quench the Spirit.
—1 THESSALONIANS 5:19

Prophetic Point

Do not discourage the prophetic move of the Holy Spirit because of past abuses or imbalances.

Paul gives us very specific instructions to not quench the Holy Spirit. The Message Bible phrases it this way: *"Don't suppress the Spirit."* Many churches are hesitant to allow the operation of the gift of the Holy Spirit in their midst. Their rationale for this inactivity is that everything must be done "decently and in order" (see 1 Corinthians 14:40). The critical question is: Whose order are we following, ours or God's? A cemetery has order, but there is no life. Likewise, a maternity ward has order, but it is a different kind of order. It gets messy. It can be uncomfortable. However, the fruit is life.

Make Application

We need to be careful that in our pursuit of "order," we are not simply exalting the familiar or comfortable. When the gifts of the Spirit are operating through people, there are bound to be some problems.

The prophetic can be messy. This is why Paul devotes two chapters in First Corinthians to help believers navigate the operation of the gifts. His solution was *never* to shut them all down and completely reject them—not at all! Paul implores us to earnestly desire the spiritual gifts, especially the prophetic gifts, which would be at work in our lives and in the church. The manifestations of these gifts are true signs of life testifying of the Spirit's Presence in our midst.

Take Action

What do you think it looks like to "quench" or "suppress" the prophetic in your life? How can you avoid this?

Ask the Holy Spirit: "What is holding me back from completely opening my heart to You and allowing *You* to release Your gifts in and through my life?" If the Holy Spirit brings anything to mind, it is for the purpose of setting you free and positioning your heart to be ready for what He wants to do through you.

Day Seventeen

Don't Forbid the Prophetic

Do not despise prophetic utterances.
—1 Thessalonians 5:20

Prophetic Point

Not all prophecies are false prophecies; not all prophets are false prophets.

Due to a lack of understanding, there are many who assume that *all* prophetic utterances should be rejected. They embrace an attitude that *despises* prophecies, similar to what Paul cautioned. This rejection typically is the result of experiencing an abuse that comes in the name of prophetic ministry. We need to learn how to appropriately heal from these wounds, separating the abuse from the truth. Just because the prophetic was abused, this does not give us permission to reject prophetic ministry as a whole. This is similar to our stance in submitting to authority. If we experience abuse from an authority figure, we still do not have the right to embrace anarchy, submitting to no one and living without restraint. During today's session, we want to help separate truth from abuse.

Make Application

Today's session is going to be a time of healing. We are truly sorry for any person who hurt you in the name of prophetic ministry, whether they gave a bad prophecy or they used the prophetic as a way to judge and call out sin. We know the hurt these abuses cause people, which is why we want to see people free from this pain. Do not despise all prophecy because of those painful experiences. When the prophetic is operating *biblically*, it is such a refreshing life source for the body of Christ. *Prophets and prophetic words do not replace the need for a personal relationship with Jesus!* Foundationally, the prophetic should stir up a hunger to hear God's voice in a more clear and personal way.

Take Action

Take this opportunity to evaluate your stance toward prophetic ministry. Maybe you are completely new to it and are hungry to discover everything that God has for you in this gift. That's awesome! Write out your desire in the space below.

Maybe you were hurt by an inaccurate prophetic word. Perhaps you were shamed by someone who claimed to be a prophet. Instead of the word being edifying, exhorting, and consoling, the word was judgmental and made you feel guilty over your sins.

Please write down your previous experience with the prophetic and what you think of the prophetic now.

Now, ask the Holy Spirit to heal anything that is wounded or hurt in your heart, specifically attached to prophecy. Ask Him to help you *not* despise prophecy, but instead be open to however He would like to speak to you. (We are going to learn about judging and evaluating prophecy in upcoming sessions.)

Write out your specific prayer for how you would like the Spirit to move in your life in regard to prophecy.

Day Eighteen

Don't Just Believe Anything

On the other hand, don't be gullible.
—1 Thessalonians 5:21 MSG

Prophetic Point

When a New Testament prophecy is given, all believers can discern and evaluate the source of the word.

Pause here and go back and review First Thessalonians 5:19-21. As we previously discussed, we are *not* to despise prophecies. In fact, we should embrace the move of the Holy Spirit, earnestly desiring Him to activate the prophetic in our lives.

While we position ourselves to be open to the prophetic, we are not to accept just *anything* that is said "in the Name of the Lord." Many people have rejected prophecy altogether because someone got angry when a prophetic word was questioned. A stance that is hardened, leaving no room for discussion or evaluation of a word, is not correct. People are fallible. The Holy Spirit is speaking to us, yes, but remember, He is speaking to people who have the ability to accidentally misinterpret what He is saying. We can get words wrong. We can think we are hearing from the Spirit when, in fact, we are just coming up with a word ourselves. Welcoming the prophetic is not an invitation to be gullible. If anything, it means that we should be all the more connected with the truth of God's word so that we can rightfully discern whether a word is motivated by the Spirit, the flesh, or another source.

Make Application

Strive to be like the Bereans in Acts 17:11. We read that this community of believers was "*more noble-minded than those in Thessalonica, for they received the word with great eagerness, examining the Scriptures daily to see whether these things were so.*" Let's follow this healthy model. Let us eagerly and expectantly receive what the Holy Spirit is saying. At the same time, it is important to constantly be listening with spiritual ears, evaluating if the word given is according to scriptural guidelines. Not every accurate prophetic word is going to be quoted, letter for letter, from the Bible. In fact, this will seldom be the case. You are not looking for the prophetic word in the Bible; you are looking for the heart of the word. If the word delivered does not reflect the character of God or align with the greater Kingdom purposes of Scripture, it is not a word from God.

Take Action

What are some ways that you can protect yourself from being gullible, while at the same time opening your heart to how the Holy Spirit wants to speak prophetically?

Put yourself in the position of the person *sharing* the prophetic word. How can you protect other people from becoming gullible and receiving whatever you say without discernment?

Day Nineteen

Hold Fast to What Is Good

Examine everything carefully; hold fast to that which is good.
—1 Thessalonians 5:21

Prophetic Point

Evaluate characteristics of the prophetic word and what fruit it produces in your life.

Once again, God is not calling us to idly receive any prophetic word that someone shares with us. This is why it is so important to evaluate what we hear. There are two parts to First Thessalonians 5:21: First, keep only what is good; and second, reject what is bad. Today, we will focus on this first part of *keeping what is good* and learn about part two in tomorrow's session.

We cannot write off the gift of prophecy because of those who have abused and misused it. We need to have our eyes trained to look for the good, while also being able to discern bad or inaccurate aspects of a word. The solution is not believing that all prophecy is bad, unbiblical and irrelevant to our lives today. Rather, our approach should be open to the prophetic ministry while maintaining a discerning spirit toward the prophetic words that are spoken over us.

Make Application

As one sharing a prophetic word, you need to bring the word before the Holy Spirit and ask Him to clarify if the word is from Him. This is not saying you will never make a mistake or hear incorrectly. We have all dealt with this; it is part of the learning process. In fact, even when you miss God's voice, you are still learning. You are still growing. When you discover that something is *not* God's voice, you receive a greater level of discernment to recognize when God is speaking and when He is not. When you know that something is *not* from God, you actually grow in confidence when it comes to evaluating the source of a prophetic message. Every mistake gives you clearer and clearer vision of what is God speaking.

Take Action

Take a moment to consider a time when you felt like the Lord told you to do something, you obediently stepped out and did it…only to find out you were wrong.

First, give yourself grace; God does! Second, celebrate the mistake as an opportunity to learn how to hear God's voice in a much clearer way.

When you heard God incorrectly, stepped out, and made a mistake, what did your mistake actually teach you about hearing God's voice *correctly*?

Day Twenty

Just Flush

Throw out anything tainted with evil.
—1 Thessalonians 5:22 MSG

Prophetic Point

Develop a refuse gate for inaccurate prophetic words.

We need to learn what to do when we receive a prophetic word—receive it, reject it, or shelve it. A word worth receiving resonates with our spirit. When someone shares it with us, there is a sense of confirmation in our heart. There may even be a physical feeling like an overwhelming sense of agreement with what is being said. The word calls the destiny and purpose out of us. There are also prophetic words that go past the mind and are aimed directly at the spirit. A word may not make sense to our natural mind; it may involve something that we have no expertise in, however, the prophetic word resonates deeply with our spirit. When this is the case, we may need to put the word on the "shelf" for a while, until we receive greater clarity and understanding about what God is doing in that situation.

Make Application

When there is an inaccurate prophetic word, there may be characteristics of fear, judgment, condemnation, anxiety, hopelessness, or confusion attached to it. These things are not found in the heart of God for us. This is why we need to develop a refuse gate. When a word does not confirm with our spirit and it actually carries characteristics that do *not* reflect God, we need to just "flush" it. Because we are all human and can make mistakes, there is strong likelihood that at some point we will both give and receive an inaccurate prophetic word. If we receive a prophecy that is inaccurate, learn how to immediately reject it. Just because someone says that they have a prophetic word does *not* mean, by default, the word is accurate! A lack of evaluation has turned many away from prophetic ministry in the past. There was the assumption that all words must be accurate and therefore heeded. This is not the case. And again, just because someone shares an "off" word does not mean that he or she is a false prophet. Yes, there are false prophets out there, but there are also men and women who love God, are learning how to hear the Holy Spirit's voice, and will make mistakes in sharing what they believe God is saying.

So, recognizing that mistakes can happen, how do we position ourselves? It requires grace. It demands discernment.

Take Action

Come up with a plan in the space below for how you can build a refuse gate for rejecting inaccurate prophetic words. Consider the following in your plan:

1. How to respond to a person who is giving you an inaccurate word.
2. How *you* can respond if *you* are the one who gave the inaccurate word.

3. How to ask for constructive feedback *after* giving someone a prophetic word to evaluate its accuracy.

If you desire to operate in prophetic ministry, the possibility of inaccurate words will come with the territory. Developing a plan will give you clarity on how to effectively respond when this happens in your life or ministry.

For Additional Study

Judging Prophecy

Available at: https://shop.ibethel.org/products/judging-prophecy-6-00pm-august-08-2010.

SESSION FIVE

Receiving and Ministering in the Gift of Prophecy

The gifts of the Holy Spirit are gifts, not rewards. We do not receive the Holy Spirit's gifts because of our good behavior, noble efforts, or religious works. They are supernatural gifts that are released and imparted purely by grace.

Summary

Discover how to receive the gifts of the Holy Spirit. Because they are grace gifts, we receive them completely by God's unmerited favor. Our works or efforts are not responsible for unlocking these gifts; we can receive them by asking, and also through the laying on of hands in the form of impartation. We can experience an increase of the gifts operating in our lives as we faithfully steward what God has already entrusted to us.

Basic Training for the Prophetic Ministry manual

Read Chapter 6.

Video Session

1. We receive the gifts of the Spirit through ________ and impartation.
2. We unlock the gifts of the Spirit in our own lives by being around those who flow in the gifts; we receive ________ from them.

Keys to Activating and Ministering in the Prophetic

1. Be faithful to ________ what you already have.

2. You do not have to be ________ to be powerful.

3. Prophesy in ________ under the influence of God's grace.

Discussion Questions

1. What are two ways that you can receive the gifts of the Holy Spirit?
2. Describe how you understand *impartation*. How can God impart spiritual gifts to you?
3. Explain the difference between the gifts of Christ (from Ephesians 4:7-13) and the gifts of the Holy Spirit (from 1 Corinthians 12, 14).
4. How does your faith play a role in how you receive God's gifts?
5. Go around and ask different people in the group how they define *grace*.
6. Based on what Kris shares in the session, explain how you have a more full understanding of grace—not just exclusive to receiving salvation, but also living a supernatural Christian life.
7. Describe the three keys to activate and minister in the prophetic.
8. Ask group members to share the testimony of how they personally received the gifts of the Spirit.

Activation Exercise: Ask for the Gifts, Impartation

Feel free to use the below prayer as a template. As a group, pray together:

Holy Spirit, we ask You to release and impart Your gifts in our lives. It is by grace that we are saved, and it is by grace that we receive Your gifts.

We don't earn them.

We don't work for them.

We don't deserve them.

But You are a good Father. You give good gifts to Your sons and daughters. So Father, we ask for You to release those good gifts in us and through us.

Help us to be more effective ambassadors of Your Kingdom and representatives of Jesus as we move in these gifts.

In Jesus's name, amen.

- Following that prayer, evaluate what God is doing in your group.
- If you feel like the Holy Spirit is sharing a prophetic word with you, let your group/class leader know so you can share it.
- Maintain an attitude of expectancy. You asked for the gifts and, because you asked, you received. You may not have felt anything right there and then, but you may start operating in the gifts in the near future. Be on the lookout for any trace of God's supernatural activity in your life throughout the week.

Day Twenty-One

The Father's Good Gifts

If you then, being evil, know how to give good gifts to your children, how much more will your heavenly Father give the Holy Spirit to those who ask Him?
—Luke 11:13

Prophetic Point

The Father only has good gifts to give you.

Many believers are concerned that by receiving the Holy Spirit, they might actually be receiving something negative. While most of us acknowledge that the Spirit of God lives inside of us because of salvation, when it comes to experiencing *more* of His supernatural activity in our lives, we can hesitate. Jesus calmed these fears by reminding us that the Spirit, who is called the Promise of the Father (see Luke 24:49), is a good gift. When we earnestly desire to operate in the prophetic gifts, we are not seeking a negative thing. It is not evil; it is not sinister. The devil is not hiding in the gifts of the Spirit, just waiting for us to ask for them and then able to overwhelm us with some evil influence. This hesitation to pursue the gifts is a great deception. The Holy Spirit and His gifts are good because they are given to us by a good Father.

Make Application

Before you ask for the gifts of the Holy Spirit to be released in your life—particularly prophecy—you need to know they are *good* gifts.

Take Action

Ask the Holy Spirit: "What do I believe about Your gifts? Am I passive toward them? Do I believe in them, but do not operate in them? Do I desire them as passionately as I should?"

Evaluate where you stand concerning the gifts.

Tomorrow we are going to *ask* for the gifts. Today, remind yourself that the Giver of all gifts is faithful. Meditate on His goodness. Trust that every gift He wants to release into and through you is good because *He* is good.

Write out a prayer that expresses your understanding of the goodness of the Father. It is important for you to meditate on the nature of God, because the gifts will carry the qualities of the Father.

If we do not believe the Father is good and we think He actually wants to pull the carpet out from under us, we will have a difficult time trusting in His gifts. However, if we see Him as one who only gives *good gifts* (see James 1:17), we will be confident that the gifts of the Spirit are good.

Day Twenty-Two

Ask and You Will Receive

Ask, and it will be given to you; seek, and you will find; knock, and it will be opened to you.
—Matthew 7:7

Prophetic Point

We receive the gifts of the Spirit through asking.

So, why do we need to ask God to release the gifts to us? After all, does not Jesus say that the "*Father knows what you need before you ask Him*" (Matthew 6:8)? The same Jesus who reminds us that God *already knows* what we need before we ask Him still calls us to ask. Consider for a moment what the process of *asking* actually reveals. Asking is an expression of our hunger. We are not content to just idly wait around for the gifts to someday be released if God so wills it. Paul reminds us to earnestly desire the gifts. When we ask for them, we are earnestly desiring to receive and move in them. Asking also reveals our absolute dependence upon God. When we ask God, we are acknowledging Him as the only One who can meet our needs, bring an answer, or release the gifts. We cannot do it in our own strength or ability; we *need* God. Finally, asking reveals true humility. Dependent people are those who live in humility, for they are mindful that God is the One who has the gifts and releases them to us. We humbly recognize the Father as the Giver and us as the receivers. We cannot just work up the gifts through an emotional frenzy. We cannot manufacture them. This is what gets people into trouble. They try to step out in front of God's leading, attempting to move in the gifts without coming before the Father as the provider. Let us ask, *expecting* to receive from our good Father.

Make Application

God is a good Father. He only has good gifts to release to us. The question is, *how do we receive them?* By asking. This is where it begins. When we ask, we are lifting our eyes to the only One who can release the gifts of the Spirit to us.

Take Action

Ask God to release the gifts of the Spirit in your life today. Perhaps you are already operating in the gifts to some degree.

In your life and ministry, describe up to this point *how* you have personally operated in the prophetic gifts of the Spirit. At what level are they operating in your life (low, medium, high)?

Celebrate what you received and where you are in this journey, but also cry out for more. Earnestly desire every gift that the Holy Spirit wants to release into you so that you can become a more effective ambassador for Christ, reconciling the lost world to God.

Day Twenty-Three

Impartation

For I long to see you so that I may impart some spiritual gift to you, that you may be established.
—Romans 1:11

Prophetic Point

We unlock the gifts of the Spirit in our own lives by being around those who flow in the gifts; we receive impartation from them.

The author of Hebrews reminds us that the doctrine of laying on of hands is actually an *elementary teaching* about Christ (see Hebrews 6:1-2). This is how impartation is expressed. So, why is impartation a key part of unlocking the gifts in your life? Something supernatural happens when you get around a person who is already moving in the gifts. There is a magnification when that person lays hands on you and prays for that very gift to be released through your life. Understand this: Impartation is *not* about someone giving you a greater measure of the Holy Spirit in your life. No human being is qualified to do that. Because of the work of Jesus and Jesus alone, you have received *all* of the Holy Spirit's Presence. Yes, there are varying degrees of His manifestation and different levels to which His power is demonstrated through us, but there are not different quantities. We receive one Holy Spirit, period. This is because Holy Spirit is a Person, not a substance. Impartation is not about you receiving the Spirit, or even His gifts, per se. It is about that person, filled with God's Presence, activating and releasing something inside of you.

Make Application

Think about people you know who move in the gifts of the Holy Spirit. Consider different individuals who authentically operate in a prophetic gifting. Yes, the gifts come through asking and, of course, the Holy Spirit can release these gifts to and through you without the aid of any person. At the same time, there is a supernatural level of effectiveness that tends to be released through the laying on of hands and impartation.

Take Action

Write down people you know in your life who authentically operate in the prophetic gifts.

These are people with whom God might want to connect you. Be open to approaching them and asking for them to lay hands on you to release the prophetic gifts.

You can also receive a measure of impartation simply by sitting under the teaching and ministry of prophetic leaders. This can be by watching videos, listening to audio, and even reading books. In the space below, I encourage you to write down a list of leaders and resources you can start receiving from.

ꕥ DAY TWENTY-FOUR

Receive According to Your Faith

Since we have gifts that differ according to the grace given to us, each of us is to exercise them accordingly: if prophecy, according to the proportion of his faith.
—ROMANS 12:6

Prophetic Point

We use the gifts in proportion to how much faith we have.

This faith principle is especially relevant when it comes to impartation and prophetic activation. When we receive from someone's prophetic gift, it is important that we come with a heart of faith, *ready* to receive from what they are sharing. The grace you receive determines the gifts you receive. Often, what we walk away with is in proportion to the attitude of expectancy that we carry. As an example, two people can sit next to each other in a meeting. One receives great revelation and impartation, while the other does not. The issue is not the level of prophetic anointing that is flowing in the meeting. Rather, it is a faith issue. There is a disconnect in one person's level of expectation. As we press in to activate the prophetic gifting in our lives and continue to receive from those who walk in a prophetic anointing, it is critical to protect the posture of our hearts, guard our faith, and always be ready to receive *abundantly*.

Make Application

Ensure that your levels of faith and expectation are high as you call out for the prophetic gift. Sometimes people wonder why they had hands laid on them, but they are not seeing a new level of anointing or gifting in their lives. This lack of breakthrough tends to be the result of low expectation. When one's faith is strong, there may not even be the need to have hands laid on you to receive impartation. On the other hand, when faith is weak, you could have the most reputable prophet in the world lay hands on you and *still* not operate at an increased level of gifting.

Come hungry. Come expectant. Ultimately, you do not receive from a man or woman but from God Himself. The person delivering the message is a person who has been entrusted by God with a gift or an office that is designed to *equip you* to become more mature in your faith.

Take Action

Consider your history with impartation. If you have had different leaders pray for you and impart gifts to you in the past, describe the result of these impartation experiences:

Based on these experiences, describe the relationship between your level of expectation/faith and what you received through that person.

Day Twenty-Five

Celebrate and Steward What You Already Have

For to everyone who has, more shall be given, and he will have an abundance.
—Matthew 25:29

Prophetic Point

Be faithful to use what you already have.

Jesus's parable of the talents is a perfect example of how to increase in any gift you receive from God. The Kingdom operates by this principle of stewardship. Increase comes to those who take what they are given and use it well. How well we use what we receive influences how God responds to our desire for more. If we are waiting to prophesy flawlessly *before* we step out and share what the Holy Spirit has prompted, then we will never use what we have already received. In turn, we will not experience increase in the gift. Do not wait until the gift of prophecy is fully developed before stepping out and sharing what the Spirit of God is saying.

Make Application

God desires to increase the activity and flow of His gifts in your life. Position yourself for more by starting to use what you already have. You do not have to be perfect. Also, do not be overwhelmed by your failures or mistakes. In fact, how we respond to our mistakes is an important factor in whether or not we are ready to receive increase. If we let our mistakes overwhelm us so that we stop taking risks, we draw back from receiving more. As we allow mistakes to help teach us, we will continue to risk. The disciples failed on several occasions—and in really major ways—but they still went on to change the world. Do not disqualify yourself from being used in the prophetic because of mistakes or failures. Use each one as a teaching opportunity for you to connect with God, and then continue to step out in risk.

Take Action

How have you responded to failure in the past specifically related to taking risks in delivering prophetic words?

Write down some ways you can use what you have already received. Get practical. Ask the Holy Spirit to show you people to whom you can start prophesying in your everyday life.

Begin to cultivate a lifestyle where every day you ask the Holy Spirit to show you specific people who need a word from Him.

ꟷ SESSION SIX

Prophetic Etiquette

You have learned what New Testament prophecy looks like.
You have discovered the keys to receiving the gifts
of the Holy Spirit and activating the prophetic.
Now, it is time to understand how prophetic ministry
should practically operate in your everyday life.

Summary

Often, resulting from observing abuses or poor etiquette, people can adopt misconceptions about prophecy. These misconceptions can take root when we do not follow clear biblical guidelines for prophecy. Both the message and delivery of prophetic words need to reflect the foundational themes of God's Word, including love, honor, redemption, and grace.

Basic Training for the Prophetic Ministry manual

Read Chapter 7.

Video Session

Guidelines for Prophetic Ministry

1. Manage yourself when you receive a prophetic word; you have the ability to ________ and be responsible for your actions.

2. Just because you feel or sense God's __________, it does not mean you need to immediately respond and react.

3. When you feel God's Presence and hear Him speak, you have a responsibility to ________ yourself.

Core Values for Prophetic Ministry

1. Prophetic ministry should be ________.

2. Do not prophesy when you are ________.

3. Do not prophesy about a ________ that you angry about.

4. Prophecy should not be a platform for our personal ________.

5. Prophecy is not a substitute for ________.

6. You do not have to say "Thus says the ________" for a word to be prophetic.

7. You are not just expressing the word of the Lord; you are also communicating the ________ of the Lord.

8. Be careful when sharing prophetic ________.

9. You are not qualified to deliver prophetic __________; only God judges.

Discussion Questions

1. Read First Corinthians 14:32. What does this Scripture tell you about the need for order when moving in the prophetic gifts?

2. Discuss what it looks like to "pastor" yourself when receiving a prophetic word. Talk about some of the misconceptions people have about receiving a prophecy—namely, that they will *not* be able to control how they act as they receive or share a prophetic word.

3. Review some protocols that people should follow when receiving and sharing a prophetic word—either individually (in a one-on-one setting) or corporately (to a gathering of people).
4. What does this mean? "Prophetic ministry should be redemptive."
5. Why is it important that you *don't* prophesy out of anger? What could this do to the message?
6. Explain the following statement: "Prophecy is not a substitute for discipleship."
7. How do you communicate *both* the word and the *tone* of the Lord through prophecy?
8. Why is it important that you do not pass prophetic judgments?
9. What can you tell about a person by the way they prophesy?

Activation Exercise: Practice the Order of Sharing Prophetic Words

You are entering into a type of laboratory. This is a judgment-free zone; the goal is simple—learn how to recognize when the Holy Spirit is speaking to you and what to do when He does.

Pray, Wait, and Receive

- Take a few moments to pray and invite the Holy Spirit to move.
- Ask the Holy Spirit to stir your faith so that you can operate more effectively in the prophetic ministry.
- Now, pray to receive prophetic words of exhortation, edification, and consolation for your fellow class members.
- Your group leader will take it from here.

What is the goal of this exercise? You will learn keys to receive, evaluate, and share a prophetic word. In addition, as a recipient, you will learn how to discern if the prophetic word testifies with your spirit.

DAY TWENTY-SIX

Self-Control and the Prophetic

And the spirits of prophets are subject to prophets.
—1 CORINTHIANS 14:32

Prophetic Point

Manage yourself when you receive a prophetic word; you have the ability to control and be responsible for your actions.

Even though supernatural ministry does have aspects of the unusual, this does not dismiss the requirement of personal responsibility when engaging in prophetic ministry. In First Corinthians 14, Paul's purpose was to provide a prophetic protocol to believers. Paul's instructions are a blueprint that contributes to a healthy atmosphere of Kingdom order. There are certain parameters that we need to follow when the Holy Spirit speaks to us. Tomorrow we will look at the concept of biblical order in greater detail.

Make Application

When the Lord gives you a prophetic word, you have control of how that word is delivered. If there are instances of ecstatic prophecy, like when a person shares in a way that it almost seems like the Spirit has taken them over, these need to be in a context that accepts this type of prophetic delivery. If the church culture and prophetic environment do not have an openness toward this type of manifestation, it will be interruptive, off-putting, and the value of the word may be dismissed due to the delivery. Just because the Holy Spirit speaks a prophetic word to you, you do not have the right to abandon self-control. You are responsible to yield to the Holy Spirit and pastor *yourself* in the prophetic ministry.

Take Action

What does it look like to pastor or control yourself when receiving a prophetic word?

Why do you think it is important to exercise self-control when receiving or sharing a prophetic word? What are some consequences of *not* controlling yourself when delivering a prophecy?

DAY TWENTY-SEVEN

God's Idea of Order

Let all things be done decently and in order.
—1 CORINTHIANS 14:40 NKJV

Prophetic Point

God and man's versions of decently and in order are often very different.

What does it really mean to "*let all things be done decently and in order*"? Unfortunately, in an effort to do things *decently and in order*, many have rejected much concerning the gifts of the Holy Spirit. As we study this topic, here are several critical points for you to reflect on. First, Paul's explanation of church order was not a rejection of spiritual gifts. Second, Paul wrote First Corinthians 12 and 14 to introduce the spirit realm, present nine unique gifts of the Holy Spirit, and provide a blueprint of prophetic protocol so that people could flow in the gifts appropriately with safety and freedom. Finally, *decently and in order* for the normal Christian life is when the gifts of the Holy Spirit are in operation.

For a church service in First Corinthians 14 to be operating in order, there *had* to be the gifts of the Holy Spirit. Paul does not present a gift-less alterative. We need to clearly understand that Paul's idea of order never rejected the presence of the gifts in operation, but always kept them in a place of prominence—especially prophecy.

Make Application

Do not embrace the *decently and in order* paradigms of others who reject the supernatural in favor of the familiar. Instead, build your life around the Holy Spirit. Pastors and leaders, build your churches around the Holy Spirit. Yes, it is important to have structure; however, instead of creating a rigid structure that cannot hold life, build structure around your hunger and expectation for the Spirit of God to move in your midst. Let us ask: "Holy Spirit, what is *Your* idea of *decently and in order*? Lord, what is this to You, because *that* is the model I want to follow."

Take Action

Describe how a false understanding of *decently and in order* can create a lifestyle or environment void of the gifts of the Holy Spirit:

What should a Christian life and a church service look like where the gifts of the Holy Spirit are in biblical operation?

Day Twenty-Eight

The Life-Releasing Power of Prophecy

Death and life are in the power of the tongue.
—Proverbs 18:21

Prophetic Point

Prophetic ministry should be redemptive.

New Testament prophecy should be redemptive and reconciliatory in nature. It is all about calling people to God, not pushing them away from Him. This *calling near* does not happen when our prophetic words are harsh, judgmental, or condemning. Tomorrow, we will look more at the reality of judgment. The fact remains that future judgment *is* coming; it is in Scripture. There is a literal Heaven and there is also a real Hell. It is worth remembering, though, that Hell was not created for humankind. It was "*prepared for the devil and his angels*" (Matthew 25:41). Scripture also reveals the heart and will of God: "*He does not want anyone to be destroyed, but wants everyone to repent*" (2 Peter 3:9 NLT). He has given us the gift of prophecy to help bring people into repentance. We know that it is the kindness of God that leads people to repentance (see Romans 2:4), so this must mean that our prophetic words should be seasoned with the love, kindness, goodness, grace, and compassion of God. Does this mean we should never mention sin, judgment, or eternity? Absolutely not! However, all of these should be presented in light of God's goodness, for it is His goodness that forgives us of our sin debt, it is His kindness that causes us to stand clean on the Day of Judgment, and it is His love that adopts us into His eternal family.

Make Application

Here are a few practical precautions to help ensure you prophesy from the right heart:

- Do not prophesy out of anger. This includes not prophesying when you are angry or prophesying about a subject you are angry about.
- Avoid sharing your opinion and calling it *the word of the Lord*. In reality, this could just be your strong opinion.
- Do not substitute prophecy for discipleship. Do not add prophetic language just so you can motivate someone to change or take a specific course of action. This is not motivation; it is manipulation.

Take Action

Describe how you think God uses prophecy as a way to bring people closer to Him.

Why is it important that you do not prophesy when you are angry (or prophesy about people and subjects you have angry feelings toward)?

Day Twenty-Nine

Avoid Delivering Prophetic Judgments

There is only one Lawgiver and Judge, the One who is able to save and to destroy; but who are you who judge your neighbor?
—James 4:12

Prophetic Point

You are not qualified to deliver prophetic judgments; only God judges.

This topic goes back to one of the basic tenets of this study—understanding what hour we live in. Only when we know what day we live in will we know *how* to correctly prophesy. First, we are not living under the Old Covenant. As a result, prophetic words are *not* the only way that people hear about God and discover who He is. In addition, a prophet's key function is not to release the judgments of God upon His people, as in the Old Covenant.

Second, we are not living in the *last day*, because that is Judgment Day. Even on Judgment Day, there will be only One who is qualified to do the judging—that is God alone. Our prophetic words are not designed to issue judgments upon people or nations. If anything, the prophetic is a tool that God has given the church to help spare people from judgment. We call out the treasure in people and speak destiny over nations because we do *not* want them to be judged. By calling out the treasure in people, we are encouraging them in His original purpose of connection. We desire God's mercy for them, recognizing the tremendous mercy that He has given to us (see Romans 12:1).

Make Application

New Testament covenant prophetic words are not about rendering judgment upon anyone. Even for them, prophetic warnings should be evaluated carefully before they are delivered. As Paul describes throughout First Corinthians 14, the purpose of prophecy is to edify, build up, and comfort. Ensure that this prophetic standard is how you measure prophecy.

Take Action

Why do you think it is dangerous for believers to prophetically judge people and nations?

Ask the Holy Spirit to protect you from a judgmental attitude. Judgmental prophecies can be a symptom of a deeper heart issue. When this defines who we are and how we approach other people, it tends to negatively color our prophetic words.

Day Thirty

What Kinds of Fruit Are Your Prophecies Producing?

You will know them by their fruits.
—Matthew 7:16

Prophetic Point

You can tell a lot about people by the way they prophesy.

In Matthew 7:15-23, Jesus talked about false prophets. In this section, we are *not* exclusively addressing the topic of false prophets. We will cover that topic in next week's session. There are many authentic, Christ-following believers who accidentally deliver false prophecies. This is not because they are apostate false prophets. Often, they are prophesying out of their own personal insecurities. In the same way that people who struggle with a judgmental attitude tend to deliver judgmental prophecies, those who are fearful, anxious, or insecure can prophesy words tinged with impending doom. The prophetic can be an outlet for their personal insecurities.

Make Application

There are some people who seem to constantly deliver prophetic warnings. What does this reveal? When the majority of one's ministry is focused on fear-based warnings, this may reveal that they hold an incorrect perspective about God. Perhaps they do not see Him for who He is truly is. Possibly they are neglecting to prophesy the opposite of what they are "picking up" in the spirit realm. As people are filled with the Holy Spirit, we pick up different messages swirling in the spirit realm. This might include the fear-mongering threats of the enemy. But when the enemy is issuing a threat or we pick up on some kind of foreboding spirit, this simply means that we prophesy against the tactics of darkness. Our prophetic words are called to *break agreement* in the spirit realm. A problem is that when people are constantly giving prophetic warnings, they can spread fear, and fear opens the door for darkness to have influence. As we prophesy, let's sever all agreements with darkness. It does not matter what we pick up in the spirit realm; let's commit to being mouthpieces of hope that declare the good purposes of God and His Kingdom.

Take Action

What can you tell about someone through the way they prophesy?

Pray for the Holy Spirit to keep your heart protected. Ask Him to reveal anything in your life that may negatively influence your prophetic words. He wants to heal you and make you whole.

Remember, God is not looking for perfect people to release His gifts to and through. They are given by grace, not through your merits. The key to accurately representing Jesus is to constantly ask the Holy Spirit, *does this prophetic word accurately reflect You, or is it being influenced by wrong thinking or a bad attitude*? Yes, gifts are given by grace, but we need to steward them well.

Session Seven

False Prophets

Not all prophets are false prophets. Not all people who share a false prophetic message are false prophets. In the same manner, not every person who shares an accurate prophetic message is a true prophet. In this session, you will learn how to identify the characteristics of false and true prophetic voices.

Beloved, do not believe every spirit, but test the spirits to see whether they are from God, because many false prophets have gone out into the world.
—1 John 4:1

Summary

There are different characteristics that distinguish the truth from false prophetic words and false prophets. Scripture tells us that *there are false prophets in the world*; therefore, it is important for us to learn how to identify them so that we are not accidentally taken captive by their influence. There are several extremes of thought in the Body of Christ regarding prophets. First, unfortunately, there are some who believe that *all* prophets are false prophets. On the other end of the spectrum, there are those who believe that every single person who claims to be prophetic is a true prophet. Both perspectives are extreme and unbalanced. The Bible gives clear distinguishing markers of both true and false prophets. In this session, you will learn how to identify key characteristics of false prophets, while also extending grace toward authentic prophets who may make a mistake by sharing an inaccurate word.

Basic Training for the Prophetic Ministry manual

Read Chapter 8.

Video Session

Characteristics of False Prophets:

- False Prophet Example #1—Spirit of __________.
- False prophets do not always have bad information; they have the wrong __________.

Three Things That Make a Ministry:

1. The : ________ Gives identity.
2. The : ________ Gives ability.
3. The : ________ Gives purpose.

- False Prophet Example #2—One who is prophetically gifted, but walks ________ from God.
- False Prophet Example #3—People who are prophetically gifted, but they do not ________ Jesus.
- False Prophet Example #4—People who build entire ministries around select, isolated Scripture verses that are taken out of ________ .

Five Tests of a False Prophet:

1. False prophets do not believe in the ________ work of Jesus Christ.
2. False prophets do not ________ to anyone.

3. False prophets need to be ________.
4. False prophets use ________ to motivate people.
5. False prophets are not in covenant ________ with other people.

Discussion Questions

1. Why do you think it is important to know the difference between false and true prophets? What are the dangers of believing that all prophets are false?
2. Describe a spirit of divination and how you believe that it is active in the world today.
3. How does the anointing ebb and flow depending on someone's relationship with the Holy Spirit?
4. What is the difference between the *office* of a prophet and the *gift* of prophecy?
5. If a prophet or someone who moves in the gift of prophecy walks away from God, what danger do they fall into? How can this position them to become a false prophet?
6. Read Matthew 7:23. *Practicing lawlessness* seems to be a key characteristic of false prophets. What does practicing lawlessness mean, based on Jesus's explanation?
7. What is the danger of building an entire prophetic ministry around a few isolated Scripture verses?
8. Discuss the five tests of a false prophet.

Activation Exercise: Discover the Authentic

The goal of this exercise is to be so familiar with and grounded in authentic prophetic ministry that you will immediately be able to recognize what is false. Studying false prophets and prophecy is not about going on a Christian "heresy hunt," where we tear people apart and devote our time to exposing lawlessness. This exercise is designed to help you do the exact opposite. You will be able to distinguish false prophets by their fruit. You will recognize inaccurate prophetic words by their tone and substance. In order to become capable in recognizing false prophetic ministry, it is important to be rooted and grounded in the truth. After this upcoming group activity, you should be very familiar with the qualities of true and false prophetic ministry.

Instructions:

1. Break into small groups.
2. Assign someone in your small group to scribe key points from this activity. These points will later be shared with the larger group.
3. In your small group, discuss essential qualities of a true prophet based on Scripture.
4. In your small group, study First John 4:1-6, as this is the basis for recognizing false prophets.
5. Now, in First John 4:1-6, look for qualities and defining markers of a *true* prophet.
6. Come back together as a larger group. Each group will share what they discovered in this Scripture passage.

Day Thirty-One

Don't Believe Every Spirit

Beloved, do not believe every spirit, but test the spirits to see whether they are from God, because many false prophets have gone out into the world.
—1 John 4:1

Prophetic Point

False prophets do not always have wrong information; they have a wrong spirit.

First John 4 gives us a solid tool to help distinguish between false and true prophetic voices. Thus far, we have looked at several different kinds of false prophets. They may be able to share accurate words, but they are still operating from a false spirit. The critical distinguishing factor of a false prophet is identifying the spirit from which they are operating. John encourages us to *test the spirits*. The ultimate question is if a prophet is under the influence of the Holy Spirit or a demonic spirit.

Make Application

It is possible for a false prophet to speak words of truth, but still be speaking from an evil influence. So, how does this work? Remember, the devil wants to kill, steal, and destroy. The devil will tell you the truth if it will destroy you. False prophets specialize in releasing fear, anxiety, dread, and terror. These are all qualities of darkness. Even if their words seem accurate, you will be able to recognize a false prophet when your spirit does not resonate with what they are saying. If there is no confirmation, edification, exhortation, nor consolation in the prophetic word, the prophet is highly suspect. Furthermore, if they fail the litmus test described in First John 4, they immediately fall into the category of *false prophet.* There is no compromise when it comes to the cornerstone tenets of the Christian faith. I repeat, there are true prophets out there who may prophesy falsely and, yes, in some cases may speak words that communicate fear, judgment, or condemnation. However, they may do this because they are unskilled in the prophetic and simply need training. Then, there are those who are clearly operating under an evil influence and are out to intentionally propagate false prophecies and misrepresent the character of God.

Take Action

Explain how someone could be a false prophet even if they shared an accurate prophetic word. How do you think this works?

Day Thirty-Two

Walking Away from a Prophetic Call or Gifting

The gifts and the calling of God are irrevocable.
—Romans 11:29

Prophetic Point

When removed from God, one's prophetic gifting can be used by the demonic realm.

People commonly try to compare prophets to psychics or mediums. The kingdom of darkness, seen in the new age movement and occult, is actually a counterfeit and skewing of God's original intention. The devil counterfeits what God intends for good. This is why there has been so much confusion in the body of Christ concerning the supernatural. The enemy's effort to warp and counterfeit the prophetic makes sense as we recognize the wonderful intention of prophecy to build us up in the likeness of Christ, as Paul explains in First Corinthians 14.

Make Application

It is essential that we stay in an ongoing relationship with Jesus. If we have a prophetic call on our lives or we operate in the gift of prophecy, we hear in the spirit realm. In relationship with the Holy Spirit, we are connected to the true Source. Out of relationship with Him, we open ourselves up to demonic influence. Let me be clear—I am not saying that by making a mistake, your prophetic calling will be hijacked and you'll be under demonic influence. However, if you make a deliberate decision to walk away from God, live with a worldly standard, and disconnect from the Holy Spirit and Scripture, by default you open yourself up to *other* spirit realm influences.

Take Action

Why is a relationship with the Holy Spirit so important in protecting you from demonic influence?

Explain how the Word of God can protect you from becoming influenced by the demonic realm. How does the Bible help you recognize truth from the counterfeit?

Day Thirty-Three

The Mark of Lawlessness

And then I will declare to them, "I never knew you; depart from Me, you who practice lawlessness."
—Matthew 7:23

Prophetic Point

Jesus warns us about false prophets because there are also real prophets; we need to discern the difference between the two.

Matthew 7:23 tends to confuse some people if they are unclear about the definition of *lawlessness*. So, is this Scripture saying that false prophets are lawless because they do not adhere to or practice what is written in the Torah, the Old Testament Law of God? No, I do not believe this is what Jesus is communicating here. Lawlessness is disobedience to God. In fact, the following verses help clarify what lawlessness looks like: "*But anyone who hears my teaching and doesn't obey it is foolish, like a person who builds a house on sand*" (Matthew 7:26 NLT). False prophets talk the spiritual talk, but when it comes down to it, they do not follow Jesus Christ with their lives. They might sit and listen to teaching, but they do not have a lifestyle of obedience to Christ. They may attend prophetic gatherings, conferences, and events, but they do not obey the Holy Spirit. They may even be pastors and leaders, but they have decided to live on their own terms, not by God's instruction. This lack of obedience is lawlessness.

Make Application

More often than not, these false prophets are prophetically gifted. They have much Kingdom potential. However, the problem is that they have yielded their lives to lawlessness. One of the most defining characteristics of a false prophetic voice is their unwillingness to completely submit to the Lordship of Jesus Christ. They may confess Him as Savior. They may even acknowledge Him as Lord in what they say, but the evidence of their lifestyle clearly expresses that they are *not* under His Lordship. Do not be deceived when it comes to knowing the difference between true and false prophetic voices. *Jesus is Lord* cannot just be a ministry slogan or catchphrase; it must be an ongoing relationship and lifestyle of obedience.

Take Action

Why do you think the test of *Jesus's Lordship* is so important and fundamental in recognizing a true or false prophetic voice?

If you are truly submitted to Jesus's Lordship in your life, explain how this will impact your operation in the prophetic gifts.

Day Thirty-Four

False Prophets Mishandle the Bible

Jesus said to them, "Is this not the reason you are mistaken, that you do not understand the Scriptures or the power of God?"
—Mark 12:24

Prophetic Point

You cannot build entire ministries around select, isolated Scripture verses that are taken out of context.

When Scripture gets into the wrong hands, it can actually become a dangerous thing. Think about Jesus's temptation in the wilderness. Satan tried to use Scripture against Him as seen in Luke 4:9-12. The devil knows the Bible inside and out. However, his presentation of Scripture will always be marred, twisted, and perverted, because his intention is to destroy. Interestingly, when Jesus walked the earth, Scripture was the very stumbling block that caused religious leaders to miss the Messiah. Was it Scripture's fault that people failed to recognize Christ? No. They simply did not see Scripture for what it is. They added so many extra-biblical laws and religious regulations to accompany it that, when all was said and done, the truth of God's Word became diluted. In the same way, false prophets make the Bible say what *they* want it to say. They twist Scripture to back up their own misguided agendas, doctrines, teachings, and prophetic words.

Make Application

Without context and appropriate interpretation, people can take random verses and come up with entire doctrines. This tends to be prevalent with false prophets, both today and throughout the centuries. I am not saying you should not teach on some of the more mysterious or mystical texts in Scripture. However, what I *am* saying is that a passage that has been debated, misunderstood, or scrutinized for centuries should not become the foundational Scripture or emphasis for your prophetic ministry. If it is, you are most likely propagating anti-biblical revelation; you are claiming a form of secret insight into verses that have baffled theologians and scholars for centuries. False prophets prefer these edgy, mystical Scriptures. They focus on Bible verses that do not have a lot of commentary or scholarship so that they can make a theology around whatever they desire.

Take Action

Describe a time when you experienced or heard the Bible taken out of context and twisted. What was the result?

List ways that you can protect yourself from mishandling the Bible.

Day Thirty-Five

"God Told Me..."

But to the rest I, not the Lord, say....
—1 Corinthians 7:12 NKJV

Prophetic Point

False prophets claim that God tells them everything; they are hyper-spiritual.

The apostle Paul received some of the greatest revelation and prophetic insight of any individual in Scripture. If anyone could boast that *everything* he said was from God, it was Paul; however, he did not make this claim. He was clear to distinguish between his words and the Lord's voice.

Be cautious of hyper-spirituality. A distinguisher of false prophets is a hyper-spirituality and exclusivity of revelation. When one claims that all of their revelation is from God and there is no space for disagreement, it reveals a heart condition. Hyper-spirituality makes others feel less than capable in their own ability to discern God's voice. They are not open to receive feedback or instruction because they have this unique, one-on-one connection directly to Jesus.

Let me be clear—we all have a personal relationship with Jesus. What causes one to drift into the category of *false prophet* is this tendency to be so hyper-spiritual that no one else can relate to or question their revelation. For example, this may look like God tells them to do everything from tying their shoes to blowing their noses. Or, even if they do ask you for an opinion or advice, they preface it by saying something like, "God told me to do this—what do *you* think?" Automatically, your counsel becomes discredited because God already told them to do something. If you disagree with them, then you are disagreeing with God.

Make Application

We know that God communicates with His people. In order to operate in prophetic ministry, we must be able to recognize and discern God's voice. At the same time, we need to be careful that we do not drift into the use of hyper-spiritual prophetic language. The "God told me" statement can be an unhealthy spiritual trump card, manipulating to get one's own way. Usually, this is a symptom of inferiority and insecurity. False prophets feel powerful when they can control or manipulate other people, and they do this by wrapping everything up in "God told me" language. Be on the lookout for this—yes, in other people, but also in your own life.

Take Action

Have you ever experienced this kind of hyper-spiritual person, where everything they said was "God told me"? How did this make you feel?

What are some ways you can avoid falling into the trap of claiming that "God told me" about everything?

For Additional Study

What is a False Prophet? Part 1

Available at https://shop.ibethel.org/products/what-is-a-false-prophet-6-00pm-june-1-2014.

What is a False Prophet? Part 2

Available at https://shop.ibethel.org/products/what-is-a-false-prophet-part-2-10-30am-june-8-2014.

Session Eight

Keys to Practicing Prophecy

One of the easiest ways to grow in and refine your prophetic gift is to start prophesying.

Do not neglect the spiritual gift within you.
—1 Timothy 4:14

Summary

It is time to exercise our newfound understanding and prophesy! This week is going to be more hands-on and practical. In earlier sessions of this study, the biblical basis for prophecy was laid. Many people never operate in the prophetic because they simply fail to step out and take a risk. This may sound simplistic, but the best way to start prophesying is to *start prophesying.* This week's exercises are designed to provide practical ways you can start incorporating prophetic activation in your daily life.

Basic Training for the Prophetic Ministry manual

Read Chapter 9.

Video Session

Practical Steps to Activating the Prophetic in Your Life

Step #1—Start prophesying your ________.

Step #2—Practice giving words of ____________.

Step #3—Prophesy over each other in groups and give constructive ____________.

Activation Exercise

After seven weeks of learning about the prophetic ministry, take this opportunity to prophesy over each other in a group setting.

Instructions:

1. Ask for a few willing volunteers to sit in the middle of the group and receive prophetic words from everyone.
   - In a small group, everyone will be able to prophesy. For a larger class, this might not be the case.
   - Encourage the volunteer (who is being prophesied over) to record their prophetic words on a phone or audio recording device.
2. Have the volunteers visit privately with the people who prophesied over them and provide *honest and open feedback*. It is important to provide this private feedback as it is respectful while also a teaching tool to improve in accuracy.
   - If the prophetic word was accurate, share how it specifically impacted your life. Be specific.
   - If the prophetic word was incorrect, share with the person who prophesied specifically why it did not resonate with you. This is a learning opportunity. This is not a time to be harsh; it is an exercise to help train people to discern God's voice more clearly and share it accurately.

- If someone was partially correct with their prophetic word, specifically mention the parts that *were* right so that the person receives encouragement.

Your Exercises This Week

Your weekly activities will focus on prophetic application and activation.

DAY THIRTY-SIX

Always Be Ready

Preach the word; be ready in season and out of season.
—2 TIMOTHY 4:2

Prophetic Point

Always be ready for the opportunity to prophesy.

Make Application

Fostering a preparedness to prophesy is a positioning of the heart rather than a feeling. You will rarely *feel* ready to prophesy, mainly because you often start out with so little. Prophetic ministry demands faith. You may run into someone at the store or come across a colleague during your workday, and all you get is one word. Initially, the extent of your prophetic word may be a phrase or a statement. Sometimes, you will not initially have a complete, eloquent, spiritual-sounding prophetic word before you need to step out and risk delivering the word. It may not even make much sense to you but, deep down, you know the Holy Spirit is speaking to you.

Prophetic etiquette is about *how* to share the word. The *when*, however, is up to the Holy Spirit...and up to you. Often, the best time to share the prophetic word is immediately after receiving it, unless the Holy Spirit tells you otherwise. Of course, you need to weigh if the environment is appropriate for you to share at that moment. But, it is important that when the Spirit tells you to share the word, you deliver it. Trust that the Holy Spirit will use the prophetic word to bless that person. If your word is wrong, receive their feedback, apologize if necessary, and learn from your mistake. Do not go into condemnation. Instead, take that as your invitation to learn from the Lord and ask Him for wisdom. Let your mistake become a teaching opportunity that ultimately brings you into greater levels of breakthrough in prophetic ministry.

Take Action Prayer

Be ready for today's encounters!

Ask the Holy Spirit to keep your heart and ears open to however He wants to speak through you.

Throughout the day, be on the lookout for people to whom God wants to speak *through you*.

Day Thirty-Seven

Start Prophesying Your Day

This is the day which the Lord has made;
let us rejoice and be glad in it.
—Psalm 118:24

Prophetic Point

Prophesy that your day is in alignment with how God sees your day.

Make Application

Many of us are familiar with this passage in Psalm 118. So, did you know that you can take Scripture verses like this and use them to prophesy your day? In other words, you can declare your day into alignment with what God desires. He created your day. Everything about His creation is worth us celebrating—and your day should be no different. You are not just practicing positive thinking or making a good confession. Yes, it is positive but, at an even deeper level, it is the heart of God for you. When you speak what is already written in the Bible, you are giving voice to God's intention on earth. God's Word is an expression of His voice. There is so much power in speaking the Word of God! Again, we are not just speaking randomly; we are not just saying what we want. We are aligning our words with God's, and when we do this we are prophesying. Similarly, this is what happens when you receive a prophetic word for someone. You are simply speaking what God is already saying about that person. You can do the same for your day. Do not just be positive. Declare what God says about your day. After all, He made it and everything that He creates is good. This makes it legal for you to say, "I declare it's going to be a good day!" You may deal with difficulties or circumstances, but if you maintain God's perspective, you will learn how to see His beauty and goodness in every single day.

Take Action Prayer

Wake up in the morning and start declaring Psalm 118:24:

> *This is the day that You have made, Lord. I will rejoice and be glad it in!*

The psalmist gave us a good example of choosing God's response rather than going by fleeting feelings. Make a decision of your will to align your words with God's. The psalmist said, "I *will* rejoice." He made a choice of how to respond to his circumstances. Similarly, you may feel one way; you might be dealing with some challenging situations. Like the psalmist, continue to move forward, prophesying that this is the day the Lord has made and you *will* rejoice regardless of what you are feeling.

DAY THIRTY-EIGHT

Practice Giving Words of Knowledge

For to one is given the word of wisdom through the Spirit, and to another the word of knowledge according to the same Spirit.
—1 CORINTHIANS 12:8

Prophetic Point

Words of knowledge are an easy place to start practicing in the prophetic because they can be immediately evaluated by the receiver.

Make Application

One of the quickest ways to start developing in the prophetic is by sharing words of knowledge. A word of knowledge is when the Holy Spirit reveals something to you that is already known by the hearer. You are not forthtelling or foretelling something in the future; you are simply revealing information that could not have been made known to you except by the Holy Spirit. Because they reveal situations in present day, words of knowledge allow you to receive immediate feedback on their accuracy. They also build faith in the individual as they demonstrate that God knows them in intimate detail.

Also, words of knowledge tend to function in cooperation with other gifts of the Holy Spirit. For example, God will typically give someone a word of knowledge about a condition that needs to be healed. If this is the case, you not only get to participate in the prophetic but also in prayer for healing.

When you share the word of knowledge, be open to receiving immediate feedback. Either the person will confirm that it is completely accurate, identify areas that are partially accurate, or give feedback that the word was off. Regardless of the result, do not be discouraged. Remember, every time you practice your gifting, you are growing in the prophetic.

Do not share words of knowledge in a hyper-spiritual way. In the video sessions, I use the example of asking the waitress for her name. You may have thought the Holy Spirit gave you her name. However, instead of making a show of revealing your revelation, simply ask her in a very normal way, "Hey, your name wouldn't happen to be Cathy, would it?" You do not need to throw "Thus sayeth the Lord" in there for any added effect. Supernatural revelation must be packaged in language that people can understand if it is going to be received by them.

Take Action Prayer

Ask the Holy Spirit to give you words of knowledge for different people in your life. In the lined space below, write down the names and words of knowledge:

DAY THIRTY-NINE

The Key to Prophetic Growth: Practice

The things you have learned and received and heard and seen in me, practice these things, and the God of peace will be with you.
—PHILIPPIANS 4:9

Prophetic Point

Basic training in the prophetic ministry is not simply about you receiving teaching; it is also about you putting the teaching into practice.

Make Application

Whether you prophesy in a group setting or share a word one on one, the key to growing in the prophetic is practice.

This prophetic teaching is new, fresh, and exciting to many of us. It is supernatural! It releases a hunger within us to begin operating at a deeper level in the gifts. Yet, unfortunately, there are many who have been taught on the gifts of the Spirit who are not *practicing* them. Why is this? Maybe we think that teaching is enough to produce change. This is not the case, as we have already studied. Obedience and stewardship are keys for growth in the Kingdom of God. For you to cultivate the prophetic in your life, you must move beyond your comfort zone and start practicing.

Throughout this study, we have had a multi-tiered approach—teaching and activation. Remember that stewarding our talents is a Kingdom key for increase. Press into the prophetic by practicing what you have learned. God is looking for those who unwrap His gifts and actually start *using* them.

Take Action Prayer

Ask the Holy Spirit to help you take the information you have learned through this study and show you how to practice the prophetic.

> *Holy Spirit, I don't want to just be a hearer of the Word; I want to be a doer. Thank You for Your gifts. Thank You for giving me new insight, understanding, and revelation about how practical the prophetic ministry is.*
>
> *I don't need more information; I need activation.*
>
> *I don't need more training at this point; I need to step out and use what I have already received.*
>
> *Help me to constantly be learning and growing—but help me, above all, to steward what I have already received.*
>
> *Show me people who need a word from You.*
>
> *Give me ears to hear Your voice, Holy Spirit.*
>
> *Give me eyes to see how You are moving in someone's life.*
>
> *And most of all, help me to take that step outside of my comfort zone and speak out what You have shared with me.*
>
> *May I always release words that bring exhortation, consolation, and edification.*

Show me how to honor and love those I prophesy over—may they feel kissed by God.

And finally, help me to find the hidden treasure in secret places so that I can call it out and help people become the men and women You created them to be.

In Jesus's name,

Amen.

DAY FORTY

Overcome Your Fears and Step Out

Peter said to Him, "Lord, if it is You, command me to come to You on the water." And He said, "Come!" And Peter got out of the boat, and walked on the water and came toward Jesus.
—MATTHEW 14:28-29

Prophetic Point

When you start moving in your gift, you go beyond what is comfortable.

Make Application

As you start to move in the gifts of the Spirit, you are stepping out of your comfort zone and into God's grace zone. Like Peter, you are stepping out of the boat and starting to walk on water. Even now, Jesus is inviting you to this new level of encounter with Him. There are new levels of grace that God is just waiting to release to you. However, your new level of grace is waiting alongside your new level of risk.

The "boat" symbolizes what is familiar to you. The "water" is an expression of a new supernatural ministry to you. All of us are on unique, personal journeys of growth. There are greater levels of effectiveness, accuracy, and power available to you. If you have never been exposed to the prophetic ministry before this study, God is undoubtedly unfolding new areas of understanding and activation in your life. If you have some experience with prophetic ministry, I believe that the Holy Spirit is calling you into deeper experiences with Him. Resist the temptation to be stagnate or complacent with your gifting. When you start moving in the prophetic, celebrate it, but do not be content to plateau at your level of comfort. There is so much that God wants to unlock to you so that you can be a greater catalyst of transformation to the world around you! The key is using what you already have and pressing in for increase. There is no point in asking for increase if you are not being a good steward of what you have received. Stewardship is your key to growth in the prophetic.

Stepping out in risk will bring you into a new level of breakthrough. The new level for you might be prophetic ministry in general. If you are afraid of making mistakes, sharing an incorrect word, or hearing God incorrectly, there is grace available to you. When your heart is fixed on God and representing Him well, there is an inexhaustible supply of grace that will sustain you as you step out into these new levels of ministry. Your new level might be sharing words of knowledge with even greater accuracy and clarity. Perhaps your new level is incorporating prophetic ministry into your workplace or business strategy. Whatever the new level is, there will be new fears trying to keep you back. Resist them. Look at Jesus and keep moving toward Him. Every new level in prophetic ministry will push you out of a place that was previously comfortable. Embrace this process, knowing that God has amazing things waiting for you!

Take Action Prayer

Pray that the Holy Spirit empowers you to grow in your prophetic gifts. In addition, ask the Lord to help you reject the spirit of fear as you move into exciting new levels of supernatural ministry.

What Is Your New Level?

After going through this course, where do you believe the Holy Spirit is taking you? It may be just starting in prophetic ministry, or it could be a deeper level of prophetic activation.

Describe your new level in the space below and keep this vision set before you. When you have clear vision that you can easily refer to, it gives you perspective in the midst of moving through seasons of discomfort. This will help you keep your eye on the prize!

For Further Study

For more in-depth teaching on *Basic Training for the Prophetic Ministry*, you can purchase the original DVD series at https://shop.ibethel.org/products/basic-training-for-the-prophetic-ministry.

This video series is your next step after completing the *Basic Training for the Prophetic Ministry* DVD curriculum.

About Kris Vallotton

KRIS VALLOTTON is the senior associate leader of Bethel Church in Redding, California, and has served on Bill Johnson's apostolic team for more than thirty-four years. He has written nine books, including the bestselling Supernatural Ways of Royalty and Spirit Wars. Kris's revelatory insight and humorous delivery make him a much sought after international conference speaker.

Kris and Kathy Vallotton have been happily married since 1975. They have four children and eight grandchildren.

NOTES